GW01463919

Brig

History Through Objects

The Compass

Steering towards the new world

Translated by Patrick White
Illustrated by Jean-Luc Didelot

VIKING

VIKING

Published by the Penguin Group
Penguin Books Ltd, 27 Wrights Lane, London W8 5TZ, England
Penguin Books USA Inc., 375 Hudson Street, New York, New York 10014, USA
Penguin Books Australia Ltd, Ringwood, Victoria, Australia
Penguin Books Canada Ltd, 10 Alcorn Avenue, Toronto, Ontario, Canada M4V 3B2
Penguin Books (NZ) Ltd, 182–190 Wairau Road, Auckland 10, New Zealand

Penguin Books Ltd, Registered Offices: Harmondsworth, Middlesex, England

First published by Casterman 1991
Published simultaneously in Viking and Puffin 1995
1 3 5 7 9 10 8 6 4 2

Copyright © Casterman, 1991
Translation copyright © Patrick White, 1995

The moral right of the author has been asserted

All rights reserved. Without limiting the rights under copyright reserved above, no part of this publication may be reproduced, stored in or introduced into a retrieval system, or transmitted, in any form or by any means (electronic, mechanical, photocopying, recording or otherwise), without the prior written permission of both the copyright owner and the above publisher of this book

Filmset in Linotron Bembo by
Rowland Phototypesetting Limited, Bury St Edmunds, Suffolk

Made and printed in Singapore

A CIP catalogue record for this book is available from the British Library

ISBN 0-670-85530-8

Photograph Credits

Musée de la Marine, Paris: pages 7, 8, 9, 10, 11, 12m, 14b, 15h, 23h, 42m.
Bernard Nantet: page 12b.
Jacana: page 13.
Jean-Michel Labat: pages 16b, 30h.
Bibliothèque nationale, Paris: pages 18, 21b, 23m, 25, 29, 32h, 33, 35, 36m.
D.R.: pages 17, 19, 27h, 34h.
Emile Ghigo: page 20h.
Véronique Ageorges: pages 26–27, 28.
Josse: page 31.
Jean-Loup Charmet: pages 32h, 40, 41, 42b, 43.
Or Information: page 34m.
Giraudon: pages 36, 37b.
DITE/NASA: page 44b.

We wish to thank
the National Maritime Museum, London,
for their assistance.

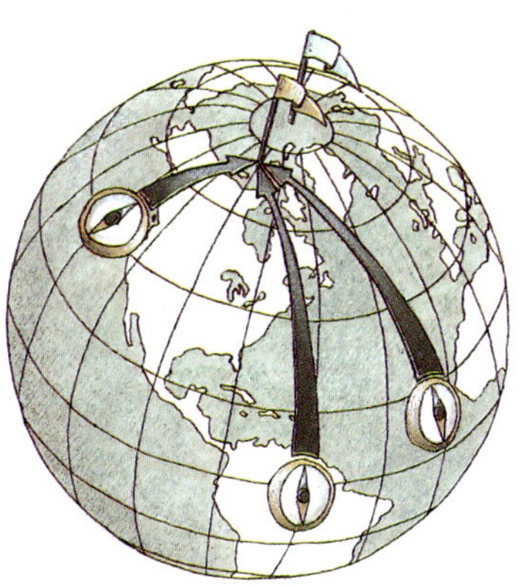

Contents

The needle and the rose

The word 'compass' comes from the French 'compas', meaning 'a circle'. The most important part of a compass, however, is not round at all but pointed: a steel needle which always points north. Without the compass navigation around the world would have been impossible. The compass first proved itself on the high seas. These ship's compasses were fitted with a compass card, known as a compass rose, showing the thirty-two points of the compass.

Craftsmanship through the ages

Despite the technical innovations made to it in the nineteenth century, the ship's compass has hardly changed at all since it was invented at the end of the Middle Ages. It has kept its distinctive form: a wooden box, usually round but sometimes square, with a glass lid to prevent air from disturbing the sensitive needle. Inside, a compass rose moves freely on the sharp tip of a copper pivot fitted in the centre of the bowl. A metal pin, known as the lubber's line, is fixed to one of the inner walls, which are lined with thick white paper. The helmsman can use this locater, which is placed towards the stern of the ship, in order to steer his course. By taking the reading from the compass rose in line with the lubber's line, he can steer a course by the compass, i.e. the angle the ship makes with the north–south axis defined by the needle.

North used to be marked on a compass rose by a fleur-de-lis. This tradition comes from Italy, where in the Middle Ages the kingdom of Naples belonged to the Anjou family, whose coat of arms included a fleur-de-lis. It seems that some Neapolitan craftsmen adopted the symbol for themselves.

Lubber's line

Pivot

A small copper cylinder, which used to have a vertical point, is fixed to the outside of the box. It was used to check the accuracy of the compass. The shadow cast by the point in the midday sun was compared with the north–south axis of the magnetized needle. It is called a variation compass.

The copper handle on top of this compass suggests that it might have been suspended in order to counteract the rolling of the ship.

This compass is 23 cm long, 24 cm high and 27 cm wide. It dates from 1690.

The fleur-de-lis

The story goes that in the eighteenth century a French navigator landed on an island where the men had this perfectly drawn flower tattooed on their skin. Recognizing the emblem of his homeland, he thought that he had landed among a people friendly to France. He was bitterly disappointed, however, as the natives had never even heard of France and had copied the design from a compass washed up on the shore.

A 'rhumb' story

The compass needle cannot be seen, as it is stuck to the underside of the compass card which moves with it. Its real name is the compass bar, a flat rectangular piece of metal whose shape varied over the years and from manufacturer to manufacturer. The compass card must be light so as not to slow down the movement of the bar. Made from thick paper, or parchment in the case of the earliest compasses, it symbolizes the circle of the horizon and carries the four cardinal points. It is graduated from North in a clockwise direction. The 360 degrees of the earth's circumference have replaced the thirty-two divisions of the earlier compass roses, each division known as a rhumb (from the Dutch word meaning 'space').

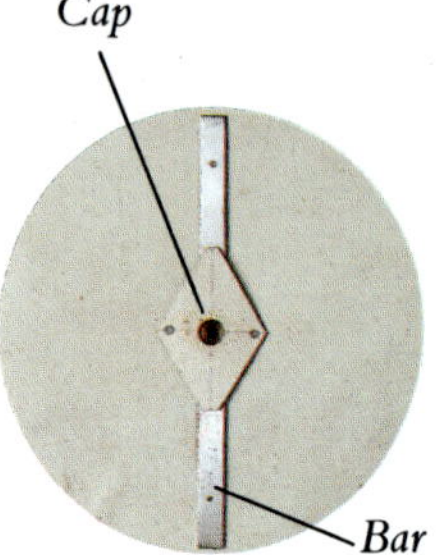

On the underside of the compass card the magnetized bar rests on the pivot via a tiny dish, the cap. Lead pellets on the cardboard diamond keep the compass card balanced.

Pivot

Almost nothing is known of the first compasses. How they were made was probably kept secret, just like the making of nautical charts. The first catalogues of merchants specializing in marine instruments date from the seventeenth century. Thus we know that the master ivory sculptors and quadrant makers of Dieppe boasted that they made the best compasses in the world. Everyday ship's compasses were made from individual parts which were assembled in port, like this one made by 'Charles Picard, master pulley-maker of Saint-Malo'.

This compass rose is decorated with female figures and sailors carrying navigational instruments such as astrolabes and hourglasses.

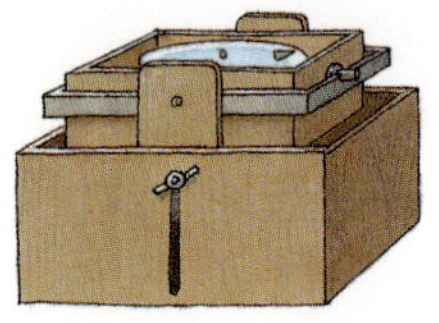
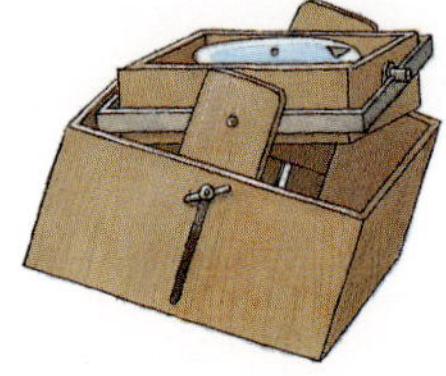

Gimballed compass which moves with the rolling of the ship

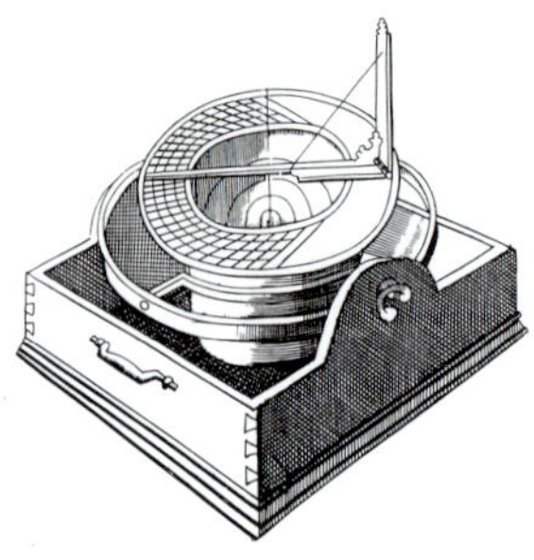

Variation compass, eighteenth century

American liquid compass, nineteenth century

The ship's compass has been gradually perfected over the centuries. Gimballed compasses were first invented in the sixteenth century. The box fits inside a frame which rests freely on two metal spindles. In this way it stays horizontal in spite of the motion of the ship. The liquid compass was invented in the nineteenth century and is even more responsive to the motion of large ships. The compass card, made from mica or copper, floats inside a sealed box filled completely with a mixture of alcohol and water.

The beginning of the twentieth century marked the demise of magnetic compasses with the introduction of the gyrocompass. It operates on the principle of the gyroscope and when animated by an electric current it moves about an axis which always points north. Gyrocompasses are remarkably accurate.

Land compass

Compass with an ivory face, seventeenth or eighteenth century

From magnetite to magnetism

Magnetite, which gets its name from the rich deposits of it found in Magnesia in northern Greece, is better known as 'lodestone'. This iron ore, which acquired magnetic properties when it was formed millions of years ago, was used to magnetize compasses. It was very expensive to buy, and each captain jealously guarded his own piece of magnetite, implicitly trusting in its properties even though he didn't know the first thing about the laws of physics which lie behind the earth's magnetic field.

The laws of attraction

William Gilbert, physician to Elizabeth I, is credited with having discovered the laws of terrestrial magnetism in 1600. This phenomenon, which extends for thousands of miles into the atmosphere, is caused by the currents within the earth which act on its core. It can be likened to a giant magnet placed almost directly above the axis of the planet, defined by a straight line drawn between the North and South Poles.

Because the compass needle is likewise magnetized, it obeys this powerful force and always lies in line with this north–south axis. However, it points to the Magnetic North Pole rather than the Geographical North Pole. The difference between the two is called the magnetic declination.

Throughout history sailors have been aware of this difference and have intuitively corrected it without being able to explain it.

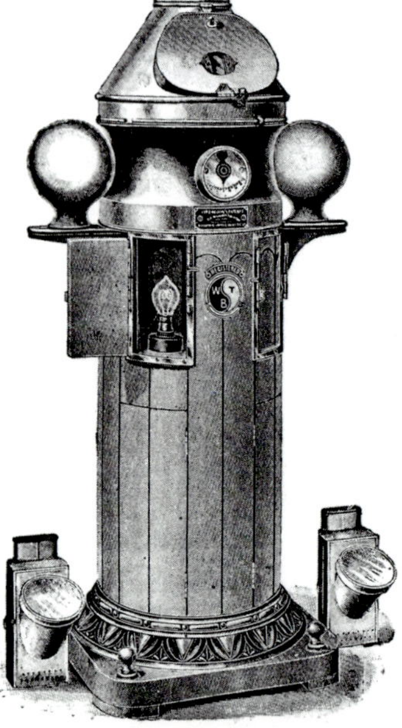

The magnetized needle of a compass reacts when placed close to iron. Although this does not pose a problem on ships made from wood, it is very significant on metal ships. To compensate for the magnetic declination, pieces of iron are placed near the compass. This cylindrical Thomson-type compass mounting or binnacle, invented in the nineteenth century, contains compensating magnets to perform this function. It also allowed the compass to be placed at a convenient height.

Before it was discovered that a magnetic force could be created by passing an electric current through an object, the only way to magnetize compass needles was to use a lodestone (a piece of magnetite). The magnetite had to be rubbed along the needle several times and always in the same direction. The lodestone was sometimes set in an expensive mount.

Geographical North Pole

Magnetic North Pole

The magnetic declination is not constant. It varies with the earth's magnetic field, from one place to another and from one time to another. These changes have been recorded in London since 1580. Then the Magnetic North Pole was 11° east of the Geographical North Pole. In 1820 it was 24° west and in 1970 7° west. The Magnetic North Pole is currently about 1,200 miles east of the Geographical North Pole. The magnetic declination is today shown on all charts.

'The stone which loves iron'

This is what the Chinese call magnetite. They discovered its special properties over 1,000 years ago. Long before European ships set sail, Chinese junks equipped with the precious magnet ventured into the Indian Ocean in search of Arab merchants.

The Arabs were famous astronomers, and their sailors had more trust in the movements of the stars across the heavens than in the compass needle. They did, however, invent the compass rose.

Legend has it that a clever Italian merchant from Amalfi one day had the idea of combining the Chinese compass needle and the Arab compass rose in a single instrument. But this is all hearsay. The only thing we can be sure of is that the compass was developed in the West some time towards the end of the eighteenth century.

This miniature from the Ottoman Empire shows the Istanbul Observatory, the most important in the Arab world during the Renaissance.

The Chinese were the first to make use of the properties of the lodestone. When placed on a plate representing the earth, a spoon made from magnetite will turn so that the handle always points south.

The north has great significance for the Chinese, being the place of supreme power. The emperor had his throne set in the northern part of the palace and the master of the house always sat at the north end of his home. So the eyes of the powerful were always looking south.

One of the few pictures of the first western compass can be seen in The Book of Marco Polo *(1307).*

The first compass afloat

The mysterious 'floating-type' compass described in medieval texts consisted of just a wisp of straw or a hollow reed containing magnetized iron and floating in a small bowl of water to keep it horizontal. Although it was extremely unreliable, this first western compass nevertheless allowed adventurers to make daring voyages. A vast world lay ready to be discovered by anyone who could keep his head and keep a straight course.

Fear of the sea

Sailors in the Middle Ages knew the sea better than anyone. They observed the currents, the ebb and flow of the tide, the colour of the water and the seaweed, which was a sign that the shore was close at hand. On clear nights the pilot would keep his gaze fixed on the Pole Star, which is always in the north, praying to God that a dawn mist wouldn't come up and obscure the skies. But how could sailors plot a course when it was cloudy, without a compass? They were better off staying close to the coast and stopping over in port, waiting for good weather or favourable winds. During these times of waiting, frightening stories were told about the dangers of the ocean. The compass laid to rest the greatest fear of all, the fear of being lost in the great expanse of sea.

In 1269 Pierre de Maricourt declared that Scandinavian sailors had been using a lodestone for many centuries. It seems possible that the Vikings, daring seafarers of the eighth and ninth centuries, knew of this stone long before the men who sailed the Atlantic or the Mediterranean.

After a sixteen-year journey through China and Persia, in 1307 Marco Polo published the first part of his account of his adventures. His stories of the people he had met echoed long-standing tales like those of the sea-monsters who crushed ships between their teeth, or of these strange men who lived by the shores of Lake Baikal in Siberia.

When they neared shore, and if they were unsure of their exact position, pilots would navigate with the aid of a sounding line for measuring the depth of water beneath the keel to prevent them running aground on a shoal.

To measure how far you had travelled, you had to estimate your speed every half-hour using a log. Logs became widely used in the fifteenth century, and consisted of a triangular piece of wood weighted with lead. The log was thrown overboard and a knotted rope attached to it was allowed to run out for a period of thirty seconds, measured by an hourglass. Then all you had to do was haul in the rope and count the number of knots. That is why today we calculate the speed of ships in knots. A boat doing 15 knots is moving at 15 nautical miles an hour.

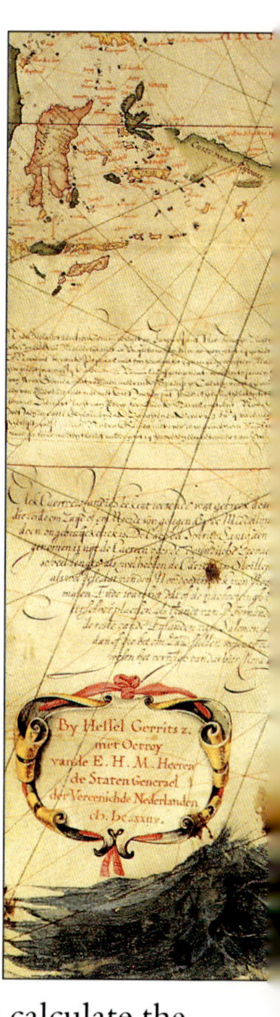

The art of navigating

Fifteenth-century navigators were not completely 'at sea' when it came to plotting a course. They used dead reckoning. Because it was not possible to take an accurate bearing in terms of latitude and longitude, two estimates were used: the direction indicated by the compass, and the distance travelled, which was found by using a log and an hourglass. On a chart the pilot would plot the ship's course from where they had set out and then calculate the azimuth (from the Arabic 'as-samut', meaning the path), i.e. the angle between the meridians (lines joining the north and south poles) and the course plotted. He then had to apply the result of his calculations, hoping that the compass was true and that the speed had been measured correctly.

This copper board is a traverse board. On each of the thirty-two rhumbs marked on it there are eight small holes, corresponding to the eight half-hours that make up a watch (each watch being four hours long).

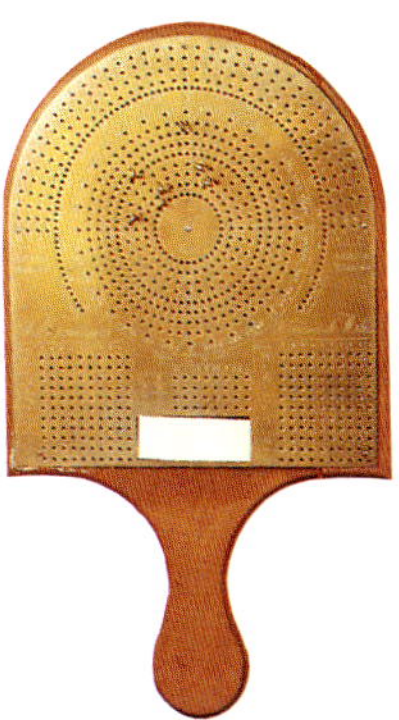

Every half-hour the helmsman puts a pin on the rhumb along which he has been steering. At the end of each watch you can then tell the course taken by the ship. The traverse board on the left dates from the nineteenth century, but this principle of navigation goes back much further than that.

Portolan charts like the one above were drawn from the descriptions of countless voyages, and show recommended courses to steer by rather than actual coastlines. The intersecting lines are rhumbs. Starting from a central compass rose, they join up with other peripheral compass roses, and so on to the edge of the chart. North is at the top of the chart, where the compass needle points. Mapmakers in the fifteenth century had never heard of magnetic declination, which explains the distortions in certain land masses over long distances. The following century a new generation of maps was invented, drawn by mathematicians and inspired by the writings of the Greek geographer Ptolemy (90–168 AD).

Which ship?

What amazing ships the caravels of the fifteenth century were, defying the heavy swell of the Atlantic! The Portuguese believed that they were the only ships capable of tacking into the winds which blew along the coast of Africa. It took over a century to develop this ship, which was to play a major part during the age of discovery. The caravel inherited the tall sturdy hull of Scandinavian ships but its narrow keel could cut smoothly through the waves. Its sails were a skilful combination of several riggings. A crew of twenty men was needed to sail it. Because it sat high in the water, it was able to explore the coasts at close quarters. But the caravel was not a ship for merchants. A more spacious ship with a more rounded hull was needed to transport cargoes of spices and the Spanish Conquistadors. And so the huge many-sailed three-masters, the Portuguese carracks and the Spanish galleons, set to sea to follow the routes taken by the caravels.

This diagram shows how a lateen-rigged ship could tack into the wind better than a square-rigged ship. It took a more direct and hence quicker route.

The front two masts of a caravel were rigged with square sails which were very effective when the wind was from behind. Triangular, so-called lateen, sails on the rear mast helped the ship to tack into the wind and made it more manoeuvrable.

Death or glory?

Shipowners knew full well that a healthy crew was more likely to reach its destination safely. Sailors had to contend with illnesses such as dysentery, tuberculosis and scurvy. Drinking water went bad after two weeks and the only foods which kept on board were dried vegetables, salted meat and ship's biscuits. These biscuits were as hard as stone and were recooked several times so that they wouldn't go off. It wasn't until the beginning of the eighteenth century that the first significant improvements were made, such as the cucurbits, huge stills designed to convert sea water into drinking water.

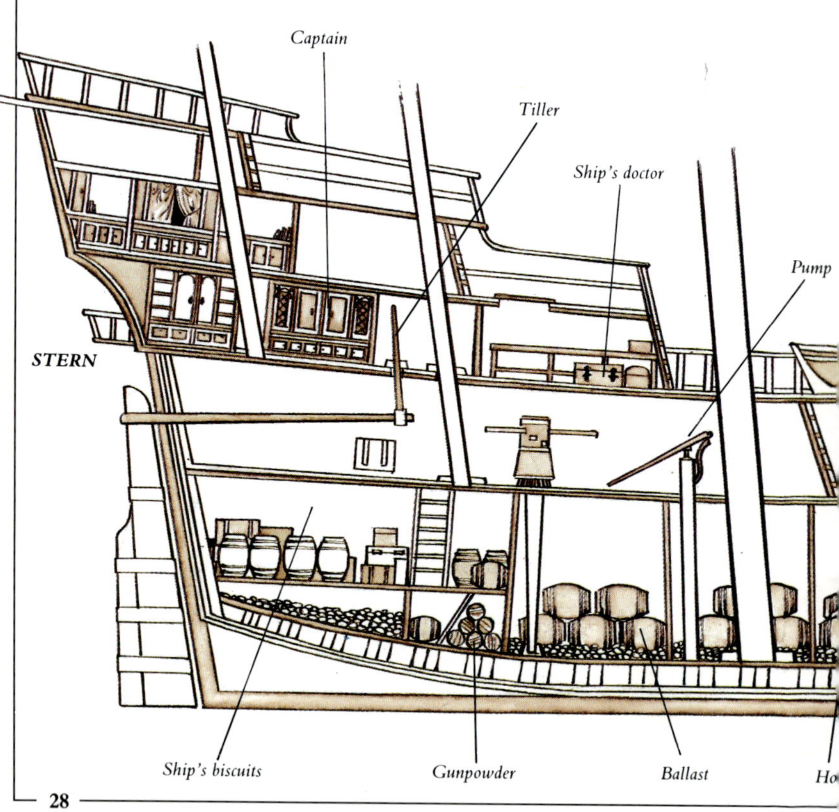

Although a ship on the open sea looked a beautiful sight, life on board was more like a 'journey into hell'. The crew, a bunch of miserable wretches recruited from fishermen and peasants, lived in worse conditions than the cattle taken along to provide fresh meat. The between-decks, where they were crammed together, were filthy damp holes crawling with vermin.

The fight against scurvy

Scurvy is a deficiency of vitamin C caused by not eating enough fresh fruit and vegetables. It was several centuries before the real cause of this illness was discovered. Vitamin deficiency first attacks the gums and then the face; it causes ulcers, internal bleeding and ultimately death. It was discovered in the eighteenth century that the dying could be cured by eating watercress. Doctors persisted in prescribing citrus fruit. In 1785 every sailor in the Royal Navy had to take a spoonful of lemon juice a day.

Cross-section of La Grande Hermine, *the ship of Jacques Cartier (1494–1534).*

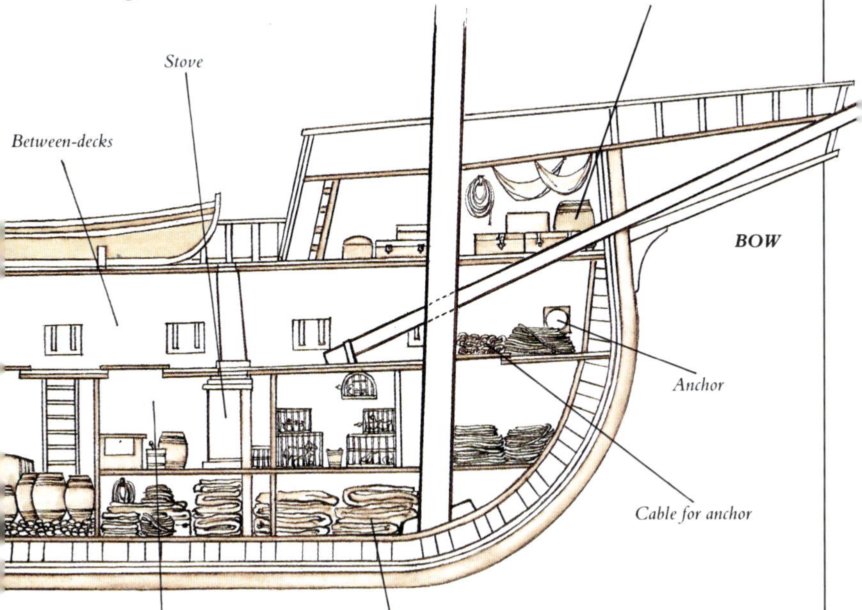

Carpenter

Stove

Between-decks

BOW

Anchor

Cable for anchor

Galley

Sails

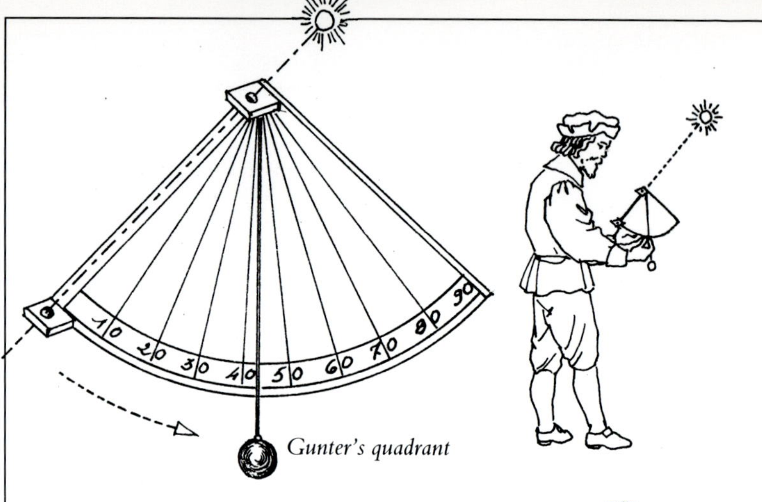

Gunter's quadrant

How to calculate latitude

The pilot measured the height of the sun above the horizon using a device called a Jacob's staff, a graduated rule with a sliding cross-piece.

With the astrolabe the pilot lined up the sun or Pole Star through two holes made in plates attached to a needle which could be moved around a graduated circle.

Gunter's quadrant similarly had two sighting holes as well as a plumb line for measuring the height of the sun.

The latitude was then calculated from declination tables.

Astrolabe

Cross-staff or Jacob's staff

To the four corners of the world

The compass, the maps and the astrolabe are stowed away safely, the pilot is at his post and the crew are a fine body of men. The ship is ready to weigh anchor. A sense of anticipation hangs in the air. There was a whole world out there just waiting to be discovered – if you were brave enough. You just had to trust in the compass needle and your lucky star to guide you.

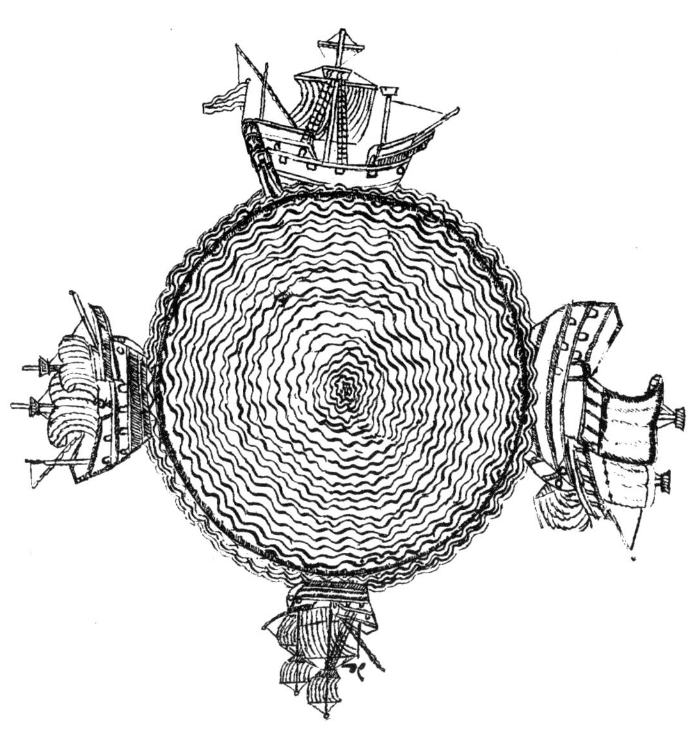

Routes to the south

The Portuguese, equipped with the astrolabe, the compass and the famous portolans, nautical charts whose secret they jealously guarded, were the first to brave the South Atlantic. At the beginning of the fifteenth century they set foot on the Canary Islands and the Azores before tacking along the coast of Africa in search of gold and ivory. In 1434 they rounded Cape Bojador, nicknamed the Gates of Hell because of the dangerous currents which drove boats on to the shore. Ten years later they set up prosperous trading posts in the Gulf of Guinea. But they didn't stop there and pushed on south along the coast, which seemed to be interminable, intent on finding a route to the Indies. It wasn't until 1487 that the navigator Bartolomeu Dias, caught in a storm, unknowingly rounded the southernmost point of Africa. On the other side of the Cape of Good Hope there awaited huge unknown oceans.

The ivory trade has existed since ancient times. In the Middle Ages the Arabs had a monopoly on the precious tusks, which were carried through the Sahara by black slaves and sold in Mediterranean ports. When the Portuguese entered the Gulf of Guinea in 1471, they came into direct contact with ivory and slaves. They bought slaves and the 'elephant's tooth' in exchange for fabrics, copper, wheat and horses. Not content with just exporting the raw material, they also had local craftsmen make a number of artefacts for sale in Europe. This sculpted tusk is one of them.

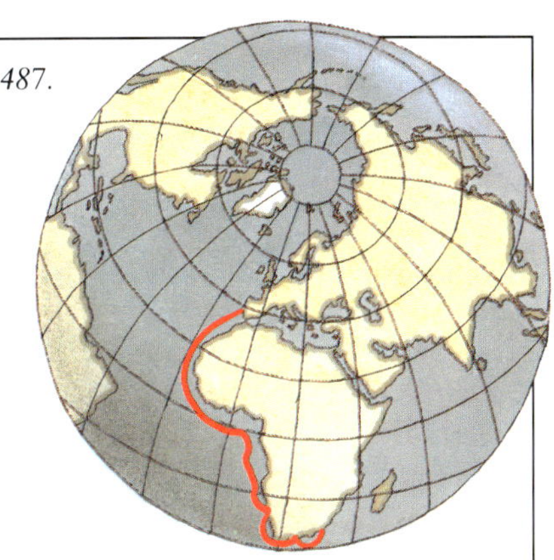

Bartolomeu Dias, 1487.

Henry the Navigator (1394–1460), son of King John I of Portugal, was the prime mover behind the first Portuguese expeditions. He had a keen interest in navigation and founded a prestigious school of seamanship and cartography in Sagres.

Full of eastern promise

The winds that blow along the coast of Africa are very strong. When he set sail from Lisbon on 8 July 1497, the Portuguese navigator Vasco da Gama chose to steer a course out into the open sea, where the trade winds of the South Atlantic pushed him as far south as the Cape of Good Hope. Many surprises awaited him. The ports along the east coast of Africa were overflowing with fruit, silks and other riches brought by Arab merchants. His mission, however, was to find a passage to the Indies, and in May 1498 he was the first man to drop anchor in the port of Calicut.

The clove tree.

When he got back to Lisbon a year later, he found that he could pay for almost all the cost of the voyage with the cargoes of spices in the holds of his ships. Exploration, however, soon gave way to exploitation as heavily armed Portuguese ships full of soldiers followed in his wake. They probed every inlet and every strait, set up trading posts and pushed on as far as China.

The overnight riches of the Portuguese made a lot of people very jealous. At Makassar on 8 June 1660, Dutch merchants after their share of the spoils lined up against the Portuguese carracks.

From the end of the sixteenth century Chinese porcelain formed a major part of the cargoes shipped back from the Indies. Made from a mixture of kaolin (very fine white clay) and petuntse (a granite mineral), the objects were made on a potter's wheel and then dried in the shade for six weeks. They were then painted, usually cobalt blue, and baked. A large number of specialized workers were employed to paint them. It was not uncommon to see sixty people working in turn on the same vase.

Christopher Columbus found a land that he wasn't looking for. In choosing his route he was influenced by the descriptions of Marco Polo.

The New World

Since the world is round, all you have to do to reach the riches of the Orient is to keep sailing west. Christopher Columbus, an Italian born in Genoa, shared this belief. He was convinced that this was the quickest route and tried for years to persuade the kings of Spain. Finally, on 3 August 1492, he set sail with a flotilla of three caravels: the *Santa Maria*, the *Niña* and the *Pinta*. He stopped over in the Canaries on 6 September and then headed west. After a long month at sea, land was eventually sighted. On 12 October he landed on a white coral beach and believed that he had found Cipangu, the Japan described by Marco Polo. In fact it was the Bahamas. Columbus didn't know it but he had just reached a huge, wild and plentiful continent.

Nose ornament, Vicus culture, Peru.

In his wake came hundreds of ships all bound for the Americas. The Conquistadors were intent on carving out a kingdom for Spain which would be so big that it would never see the sun set.

Death of the Indians

'. . . [the Spanish] behave like savage tigers and lions who haven't eaten for days. Over twelve million people – men, women and children – died in the space of forty years at the hands of the Spanish tyrants. There were two main ways in which these so-called Christians wiped these poor wretched people off the face of the earth: the first was by unjust and cruel wars, the second by oppression and slavery worse than any human being or animal had ever known. The reason why Christians killed so many human beings was their insatiable desire for gold.'

(B. de las Casas, Account of the Spanish Voyages and Discoveries in the West Indies, *1542)*

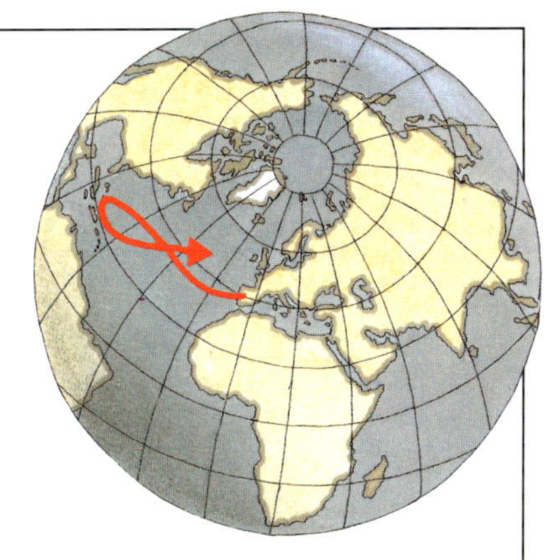

Christopher Columbus, 1492–3.

This illustration, taken from the Codex Azcatitlan, *shows the Spanish Conquistadors arriving in Tenochtitlan (Mexico) in 1519. The town was besieged in May 1521 and then stormed and the Aztec population massacred.*

No way through up north

A new route to the Indies at any cost! The quays of Bristol, Saint-Malo and Amsterdam were agog with excited talk of the spice islands. But what route should they take to get there before the Portuguese carracks? Since the end of the fifteenth century, English, Breton and Basque fishermen had been sailing unhindered to the shores of Newfoundland, where there were large stocks of fish. They were soon followed by ships fitted out by the kings of Europe, their mission to discover the famous North-west Passage to Asia. So when Jacques Cartier (1494–1555) came across the Saint Lawrence estuary he thought he had found the much sought-after route. Disappointment followed disappointment and shipwreck followed shipwreck, as these northern latitudes are not favourable to navigation. As well as the dangers of the sea, the explorers had to contend with the mist which obscured the stars and the ice which crushed their ships. No European was bold enough to brave the perpetual night of the Arctic winter.

Coloured engravings taken from G. de Veer's book Barents' Three Voyages to the Arctic *(1609).*

The Arctic winter

In 1596 the Dutchman Willem Barents risked a push to the north-east in the hope of finding a passage to Asia. After having discovered Spitsbergen and rounded the northern end of Novaya Zemlya, he became trapped in the ice. Forced to spend the winter in a place which he himself called 'the ice harbour', he and his companions survived. But any hope of establishing direct contact with Asia via northern Russia perished there among the ice.

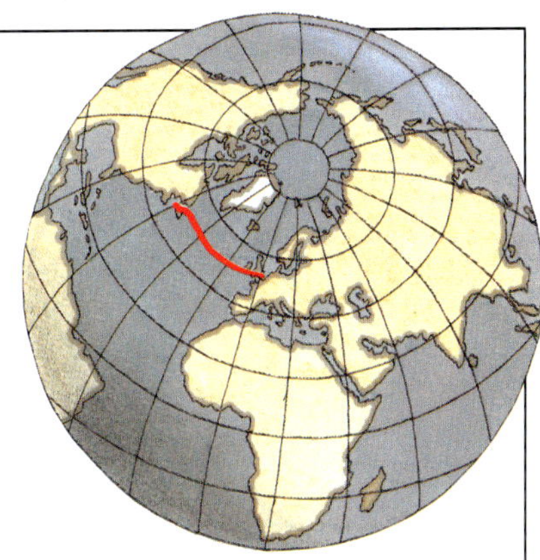

Jacques Cartier, 1535.

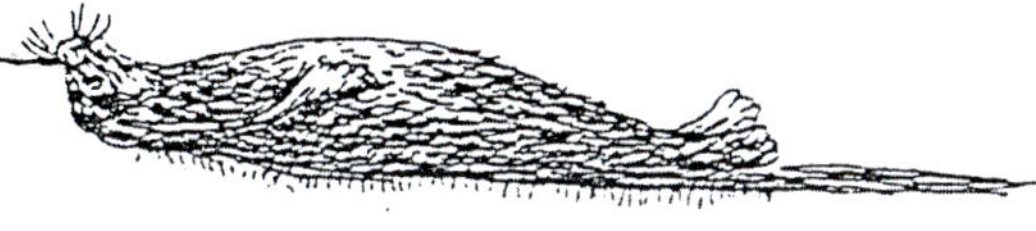

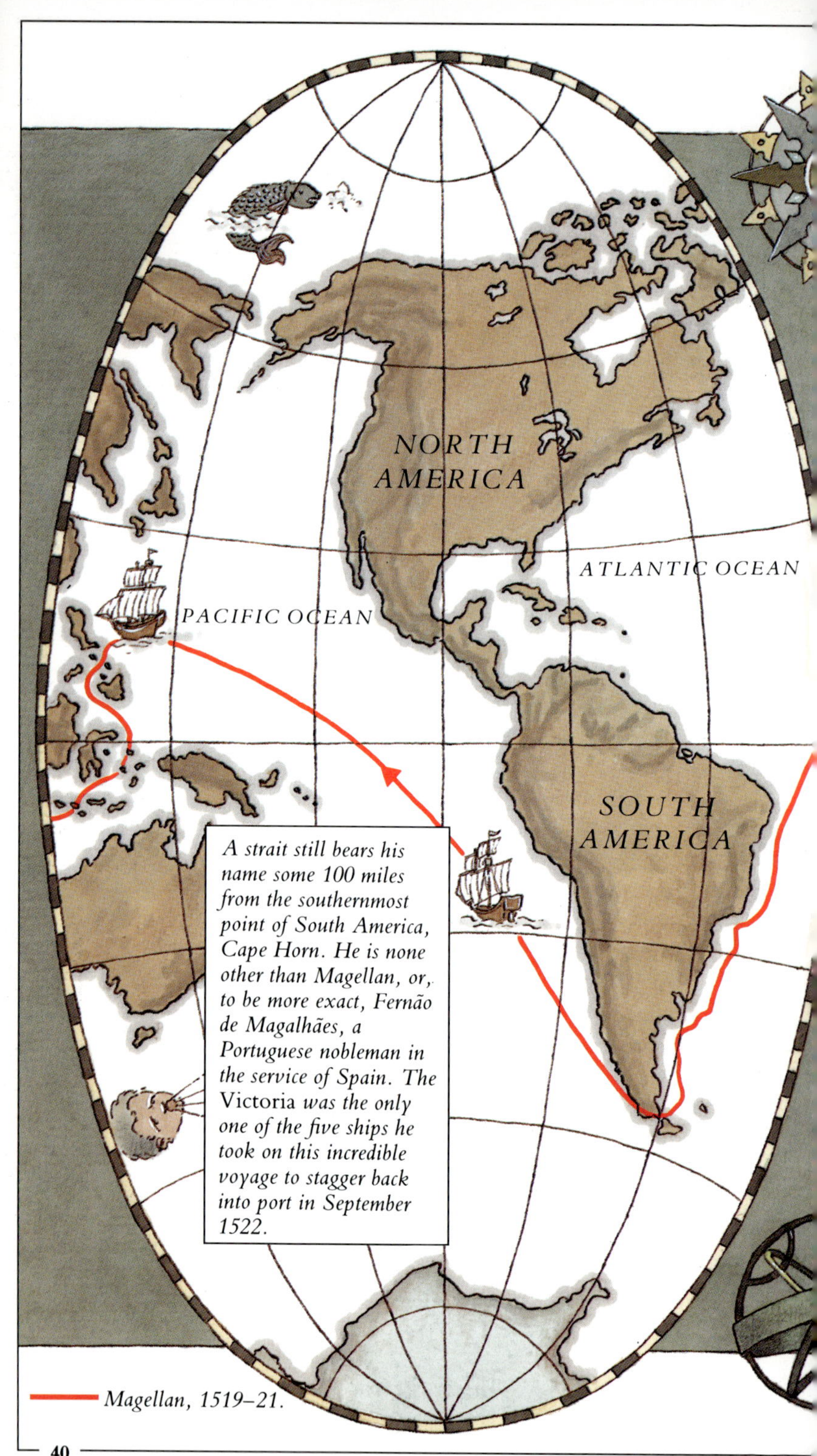

A strait still bears his name some 100 miles from the southernmost point of South America, Cape Horn. He is none other than Magellan, or, to be more exact, Fernão de Magalhães, a Portuguese nobleman in the service of Spain. The Victoria *was the only one of the five ships he took on this incredible voyage to stagger back into port in September 1522.*

Magellan, 1519–21.

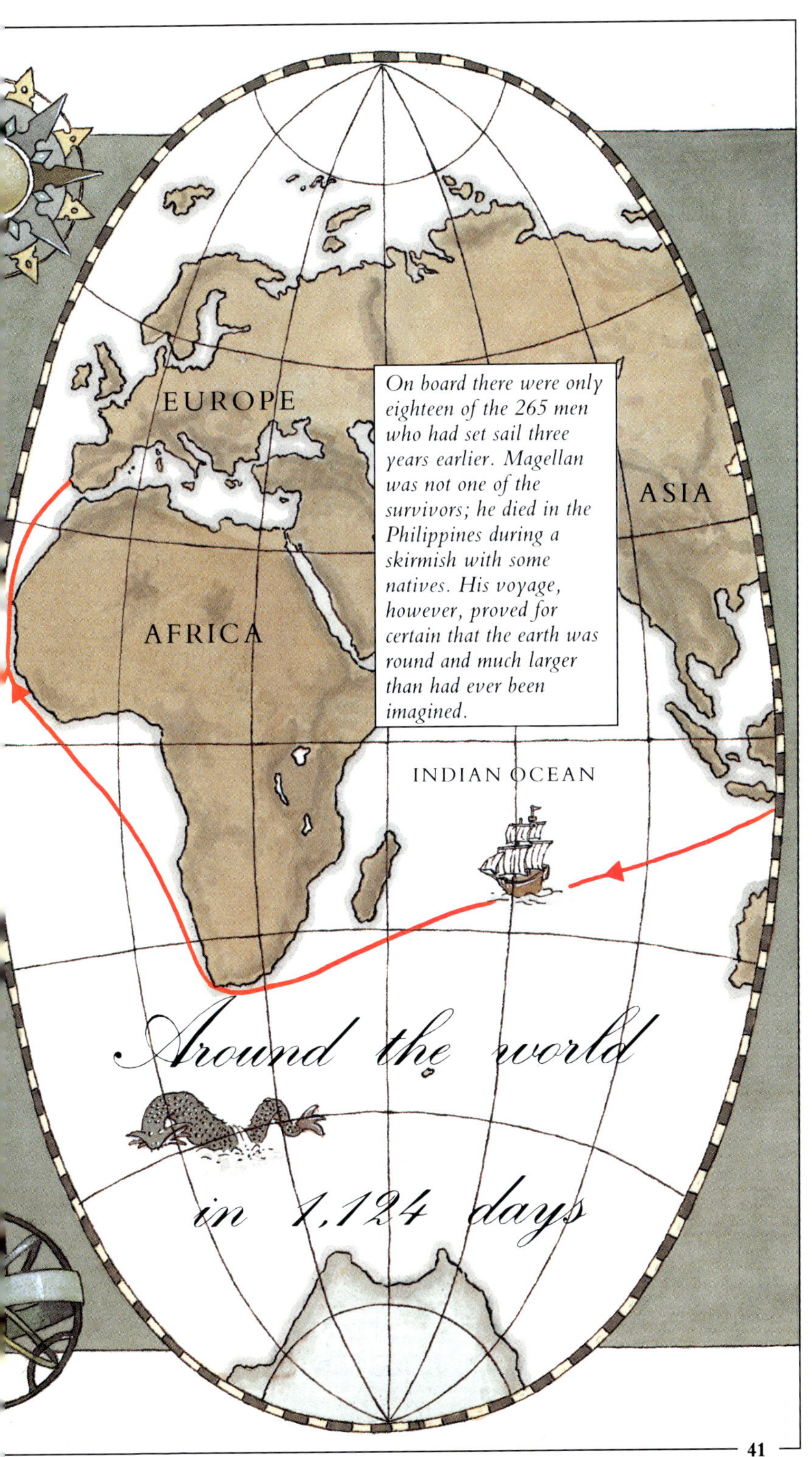

On board there were only eighteen of the 265 men who had set sail three years earlier. Magellan was not one of the survivors; he died in the Philippines during a skirmish with some natives. His voyage, however, proved for certain that the earth was round and much larger than had ever been imagined.

Explorers and wise men

New details of the world map were filled in with every new voyage. Included on this map were numerous archipelagos named after the men who had patiently mapped out their coastline. As instruments became increasingly sophisticated, so our knowledge of the world took giant steps forward. Peculiarly enough, the world maps of 1800 show less land than those made in 1500. The imaginary islands of the Middle Ages had been unable to survive three centuries of investigation. One myth persisted, though, that of the 'Terra Australis Incognita', this mysterious southern continent which was supposed to keep the globe balanced. In the eighteenth century, the Age of Reason, this myth was finally laid to rest. Only after the explorations of Captain James Cook (1728–79) in the South Pacific and the discovery of Australia and New Zealand was the infamous unknown continent reduced to the dimensions of present-day Antarctica.

Baskets for collecting plants (watercolours taken from a manuscript about the planned voyages of the Count of La Pérouse, 1785).

*The port of Honolulu in the Hawaiian Islands (*The Colourful Voyage around the World of Louis Choris*, middle part of the nineteenth century).*

Longitude

One of the scientific instruments that Cook took on his 1772 voyage was a 'machine for measuring time', or, to be more precise, a marine chronometer which could be used to calculate longitude. Until then, because there were no watches accurate enough to keep time, sailors had been able to fix their position on the globe only in terms of latitude. The principle of longitude, however, had been known for some centuries. This is how the German astronomer Regiomontanus put it in 1474: 'Since the world rotates by 360 degrees every 24 hours, in other words 15 degrees an hour, the number of degrees travelled can be calculated by multiplying by fifteen the difference between local time and the time of the place from where the ship set out'. Longitude is counted from east to west starting from a prime meridian, today the Greenwich meridian which passes through London.

A ship called *Compass*

In the spring of 1788, the French ships *La Boussole (Compass)* and *L'Astrolabe (Astrolabe)* foundered on the Vanikoro reefs off the Solomon Islands in the South Pacific. Thus ended the ill-fated expedition lead by Jean-François de Galaup, Count of La Pérouse, who set out from Brest on 1 August 1785 to circumnavigate the globe. This voyage was to be the French answer to the explorations of Captain Cook.

King Louis XVI had a passionate interest in geography. He had followed the preparations closely and had himself jotted down some advice on, among other things, how to observe the magnetic declination. The scientific equipment available to the Count showed what an ambitious project it was. The many instruments carried on board included Berthoud's new chronometers for calculating longitude, sextants for calculating latitude and variation compasses for drawing new maps.

Between 1768 and 1779 Captain James Cook circumnavigated the globe three times. He explored and charted the Pacific and the coasts of New Zealand and Australia, and travelled further south than any man before him. On his first voyage in 1770 he anchored at Botany Bay, naming it that because of the interesting plants found on its shores.

Like the sextant, the octant was used to measure the height of the sun and to determine the latitude of a ship, i.e. its position relative to the Equator.

Two officers taking measurements of the giant statues on Easter Island in 1786 as part of the Count's expedition.

Rivals at sea

At the dawning of the twentieth century, even though the Age of Discovery was long past, the poles remained a source of mystery. Hundreds of failed expeditions were launched over decades of dashed hopes and terrible suffering by men not used to these extreme latitudes. In the north the Norwegian Roald Amundsen finally made the North-west Passage between the Atlantic and the Pacific a reality by crossing the Arctic, but it was the American Robert Peary who was the first man to stand on the top of the world on 7 April 1909. He noted in his diary: 'I had passed over or very near the point where north and south and east and west blend into one.'

Amundsen then set off to the Antarctic, where he beat his unlucky rival, Scott, to the South Pole on 14 December 1911.

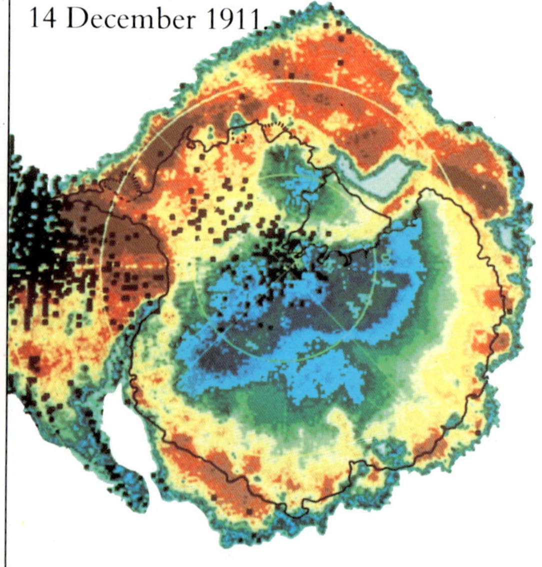

Satellite photograph of the Antarctic during the polar summer. Blue represents the glaciers.

Museums to visit

National Maritime Museum, Greenwich, London.

Imperial War Museum, London.

Maritime Museum, St George's Quay, Lancaster.

Merseyside Maritime Museum, Pierhead, Merseyside.

Maritime Museum for East Anglia, Great Yarmouth, Norfolk.

Royal Naval Museum, Portsmouth, Hampshire.

Scottish Maritime Museum, Irvine, Ayrshire.

Aberdeen Maritime Museum, Shiprow, Aberdeen.